Published by WANDERER BOOKS
A Division of Simon & Schuster, Inc.
Simon & Schuster Building
1230 Avenue of the Americas
New York, New York 10020
WANDERER and colophon are registered trademarks of Simon & Schuster, Inc.

First published in 1981
by Macmillan Children's Books
a division of Macmillan Publishers Limited
4 Essex Street, London WC2R 3LF
and Basingstoke

First American edition 1984

10 9 8 7 6 5 4 3 2 1

Printed in Hong Kong

ISBN: 0-671-50072-4

Adviser: Mary Clarke
Designer: Julian Holland
Picture Researcher: Stella Martin
Photo Credits:
Australian Information Service, London;
BBC Hulton Picture Library; Mary Clarke Dance Collection;
Jesse Davis; Zoe Dominic; Dutch National Ballet;
London Festival Ballet; National Ballet of Canada;
National Ballet School of Canada; Novosti Press Agency;
David Palmer; SCR, London; Victoria and Albert Museum,
London; Reg Wilson
Cover: Reg Wilson

Our special thanks to Lesley Collier, Antoinette Sibley,
Mary Clarke, Reg Wilson, Dorothy Humanitzki, Jesse Davis
and the Royal Ballet School for their help and cooperation
in the making of this book.

TO ████ with love
grandma + pop-pop ████ 1987!

The World of Ballet

Robin May

Wanderer Books
Published by Simon & Schuster, Inc., New York

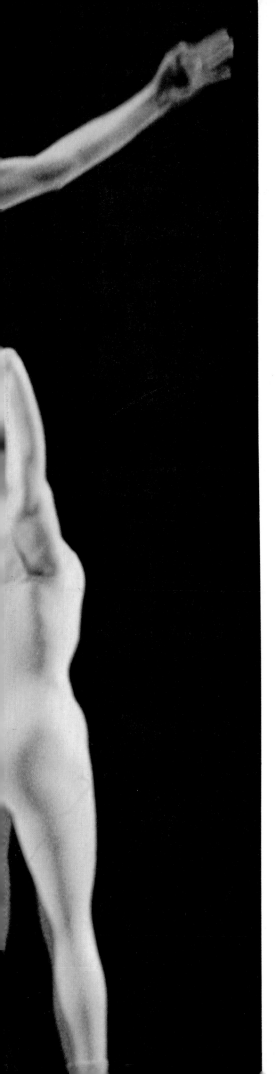

Contents

All over the world dance companies are performing new ballets. These often look very different from classical ballets, and the dancers may even dance in bare feet. The dancers (left) are performing a contemporary work. Many modern dancers have been classically trained.

Introduction

Antoinette Sibley was a star of the Royal Ballet Company until she retired recently. In the picture (left) she dances the role of Princess Aurora in Tchaikovsky's famous ballet, *The Sleeping Beauty*. The role has been the supreme test of ballerinas since it was first performed in Russia many years ago in 1890.

The world of ballet is divided into two parts – the extreme hard work and relentless exercising coupled with the magical special fantasy world of make-believe!

This fascinating book shows both these sides admirably, starting with the work in ballet school and rehearsal room, watching the choreographers at work, and following a ballerina through an entire evening from time of arrival at the theater until she leaves for home.

We also follow the history of ballet from early ballets and dancers to the present and end with the stars of ballet today in performance.

Ballet is a tremendously popular form of entertainment and the last decade has seen this lovely art not only flourish but positively explode in popularity. Ballet can fill two large opera houses to capacity on the same evening – not only in Moscow but in London, Paris, and New York.

I am sure that adults and children alike will want to delve many times into this book.

Antoinette Sibley

Ballet Schools

The Five Positions

For ballet lovers, the magic begins the moment they enter the theater. If the performance is a great one, that magic will linger on long after it. There is plenty of magic in the colorful world behind the curtain, too, but there is also hard work by dedicated people.

Ballet aims at perfection, and audiences often believe they have seen it. Behind the scenes, however, the dancers are not likely to be thinking that they are perfect. No true artist is ever wholly satisfied with his or her performance and is always striving to do better. In these pages you will learn just how tough the life of a dancer is.

It all begins at ballet school. Here, to start this book, are the very foundation stones of ballet – the five positions.

The first position. The legs are together, with the heels touching but not overlapping. The feet are in a straight line and the arms are held gracefully at the front of the body.

The fourth position. There are two versions of this position. The difference between the two relates to the placing of the front foot and the arms. The position above left is an extension of the first

position – the open position. The position above right is an extension of the fifth position – the closed position. For both of these stances the feet are placed about 10 inches apart.

The second position. The feet, still in a straight line, are about 20 inches apart, while the arms are stretched out to the side. The weight of the body is evenly distributed.

The third position. The feet are still in a straight line, but the heel of the front foot "locks" into the instep of the back foot. One arm is extended to the side.

The fifth position. The feet are brought together here with the toes of one foot resting against the heel of the other. The arms soar elegantly up into the air.

The five basic positions of the ballet dancer's feet were worked out more than 300 years ago. Nearly all the steps in classical ballet begin and end with these famous positions. Whoever first invented them wanted a dancer's balance to be ideal.

A Frenchman named Pierre Beauchamp was the first to write them down. He did so in the late 17th century, but it is likely that they were in use earlier.

The positions are very important because they must be mastered by young would-be dancers before training can start.

For every one of these positions, the feet must be turned out from the hip. Once the young dancer can turn his or her legs out 180 degrees from the hip, he or she has real freedom of movement and will look elegant.

Basic Training

You have to be really determined to succeed as a ballet dancer, and determined over a long period – all your working life. Every day, beginners and ballerinas alike start with a rugged spell of training. The very first movements will be at the barre, and gradually the body begins to warm up. In a ballet company the session will end with spectacular leaps by the men and dancing on pointe by the women.

Naturally, would-be dancers are given a very thorough medical check-up before they embark on such a hard life. It is not enough to have a graceful body. Any weakness must be spotted when the child is 10 or 11 to prevent heartbreak later on. At the age of 16, full-time professional training is undertaken. The result will be perfect control of the body so that miracles of excitement and grace can be achieved. As these pictures of students show, there are no shortcuts to becoming a world-acclaimed dancer.

A young dancer (above) in retiré, on pointe on her left leg.

A striking glimpse (above) of two young dancers working at the barre.

Our dancer uses the barre (left), again on full pointe. The beautiful pose shows the lovely relaxed curve of the arms.

Work at the barre begins as soon as the young dancer reaches her dancing school, and it never ends. A ballet class is a very democratic affair too. In a company you will find everyone from newcomers to ballerinas taking part, and all will obey the instructions of the ballet teacher.

Bending of the knees in ballet is called *plié* (below). When the heels remain firmly on the ground, it is called *demi-plié*. When the knees are completely bent, the phrase used is *grand plié*.

Strength and Grace

Ask someone in the street who is the toughest, a boxer, a football player, an Olympic athlete, or a male ballet dancer, and the chances are he will fail to give the right answer. The dancer has to reach and maintain, over many years, a peak of fitness unknown in any other walk of life.

Male students do rugged gymnastics. It is all part of the training that enables them to execute those amazing leaps and lifts, which must not only be perfect, but must always look totally graceful and unstrained.

Naturally, young student dancers have to acquire a regular education as well. The beginning student will often have to give up his or her free Saturday in order to go to dance classes. However, many of the leading ballet companies of the world have ballet schools, and admission to them is highly competitive, and only the best students are accepted. The youngsters then face years of hard work. When their formal training is over, many will graduate into a corps de ballet. From there, some will go on to become soloists or principals. Only a few will become ballet immortals.

Too many people still believe that ballet dancing is no life for a man. Few Russians would ever express such a belief, neither would any Danes. Both these nationalities think it natural for men to dance, and so do many million others around the world.
Of course, it is no life for a weakling, as these pictures show. The combination of great strength, agility, and grace is a rare one, but the male dancer has to have it. These two pictures (above and left) show strikingly something of the world of the male dancer.

Part of the training of a ballet student is gymnastics. This strengthens and prepares them for the more strenuous side of dancing. Not everyone can aspire to the feats of Bolshoi-trained dancers or achieve the impossible like Baryshnikov and Nureyev, but all achieve small miracles.

These photographs (above and right) show young male dancers going through their paces, but they will also be expected to excel in the skills of gymnastics and acrobatics.

Ballet Clothes

Dancers, young and old, must train every day of their working lives, except on a rest day or on their yearly holiday; and what they wear when practicing is very important. At the beginning of a class some will be wearing the thick, knitted leggings called leg-warmers to help keep unexercised muscles warm. These will be taken off as the dancers steadily get warmer.

Shoes are naturally especially important, particularly for girls who, from about the age of 12, start going up on pointe. There were no pointe shoes in the early days of ballet, dancers just padded their shoes with cotton wool. Then, around 120 years ago, ballet shoes were first "blocked" – stiffened with glue that gave them support and real strength.

It is the first dancing class of the day, and the dancer at the barre is wearing leg-warmers.

There must be no danger of slipping when on pointe and, to make sure of this, the dancer is rubbing the tip of her shoe in a special resin.

Now the dancer is up on pointe. Girls do not begin to do this until they are at least 12 years of age.

Mime

Mime is acting without words. Naturally, dancers use their whole body to express feelings, but some ballets have passages of mime where gestures are used to advance the story. Ballet developed its own series of mime gestures, and, in the middle of the last century, these became very significant at certain moments. Examples occur in *Giselle*, *Swan Lake*, and other 19th-century classics. In our own century, mime steadily became less important in new ballets. The change came about because the great Russian choreographer Mikhail Fokine believed that flowing "musical" gestures were better than traditional "messages" in mime. As well as the gestures shown here, there are others like See, No, Marry, and Ask. All of them are delightful.

This is the mime version of "Hear" with the hands indicating the dancer's ears. Like all mime gestures, this one is sensible as well as a pleasure to look at.

The girl is using mime to indicate fear. Note the way she uses her hands to ward off something or someone evil.

The way to express love in mime is demonstrated here. The dancer's hands are clasped over her heart. As we all know, "hand on heart" indicates love.

15

Teaching Ballet

Pupils at many of the leading ballet schools around the world can expect to be taught by the very best teachers available. For dancers love their art so much that they are only too eager to pass their knowledge on to the younger generation. This explains why the standards of the world's great companies remain so high. The very greatest artists are eager to communicate what they know. The incomparable dancer Galina Ulanova is an example. She was Soviet Russia's most famous dancer and, after she had given her farewell performance in 1962, she turned to coaching, with spectacular results. She is a supreme example of an artist who has handed down her knowledge to the young.

The story is the same in other parts of the world. There are, of course, far more teachers who were never superstars, but who were and are born teachers, makers of stars and of other dancers, who then become the backbone of companies around the world. The teachers shown here represent teachers everywhere.

Julia Farron, once a principal of the Royal Ballet, is seen giving advice to pupil (above).

Dame Alicia Markova, the first and greatest of all British ballerinas, is showing a group of fortunate girls a series of movements (below).

William Glassman (left), formerly a soloist with American Ballet Theatre, retired as a dancer in 1971 and is now a teacher of advanced students.

Lynn Wallis (below), of the Royal Ballet School, teaches a section of the ballet *Les Patineurs*, which was choreographed by Frederick Ashton and first produced in 1937.

The Corps de Ballet

The corps de ballet, like the chorus of an opera, is a vital part of any company. All ballet is teamwork, but for obvious reasons, teamwork is particularly in evidence when the corps de ballet is dancing. On these pages some of the pupils of the Royal Ballet School are being instructed in corps de ballet work by Lynn Wallis. The ballet is *Les Patineurs*, and this mixed class is getting the benefit of an expert's advice and skill.

This pose (left) demonstrates clearly the all-important value of teamwork. Symmetry of movement, timing, and the ability to work together all contribute to the success of the corps de ballet.

Les Patineurs had a very starry cast when first produced in 1937 in London. Its dancers included Margot Fonteyn and Robert Helpmann. The ballet has often been revived and is ideal for training a corps de ballet in the art of teamwork. How many of these young dancers (left) will one day be stars? In a way that is beside the point. To be a useful member of a corps de ballet is an interesting career in itself.

The teacher is responsible for teaching her students the steps and movements of the ballets in the company's repertory. Here Lynn Wallis stops a rehearsal of *Les Patineurs* to make a correction.

Other Activities

Ballet training involves more than dancing. Ordinary education must go on, and this means that along with the five positions, and everything that stems from them, French, mathematics, English, history, etc. must be learned. Only a handful of students will succeed in a dancing career, so education in other fields is vitally important.

Naturally, some subjects have real links with the world of ballet – any form of art, for instance. Music forms a vital part of every ballet, and musical understanding is essential for the ballet student. Students will also be constantly in touch with the world of painting and design, because scenery and costumes play such a key role in the staging of a ballet.

These things are all a part of the busy world of the ballet student. You have to be dedicated to start on such a life, a life that leads to one of the most disciplined professions on earth. Many would say that it is the most disciplined of all.

When they are not in dance class, many students pursue other talents. Here (above) young girls enjoy an art class.

This young dancer (left) has put her barre work aside as she concentrates on creating a piece of pottery.

Long before they make their first professional appearances, many young dancers have the opportunity to perform in amateur theatricals. Two such colorful events (above and right) show young students in performance, complete with scenery and costumes.

Outdoor Dance

Outdoor entertainment has been popular since the days of the ancient Greeks. Even today, many dancing and acting companies forsake their city theaters and move outdoors when the warm weather sets in.

Shakespeare in the open air is particularly popular, and this brings us to the pictures on these pages. The entertainment is *A Midsummer Night's Dream*, not by the master himself, but an extravaganza based on his play. Here students have a chance to perform, and when they are not "on stage," they are likely to be found helping other artists adjust their costumes.

Such group activities are fine training for every sort of theater, not just for ballet. These presentations are also a reminder that all theater descended from ancient dances.

A dance group in full flight (above) recalls the graceful days of ancient Greece.

The performers make many of their own costumes (left) and very striking they are.

A fine body of pixies on parade (right) in this colorful entertainment inspired by the master entertainer, William Shakespeare.

Young Dancers

There is a great deal in this book about the key role Russia has played in ballet history, which, of course, includes the training of young dancers. Russian ballet dates back to 1738, when the Imperial Ballet School was founded in St. Petersburg (now Leningrad). The first ballet master was a Frenchman, Jean Baptiste Landé, whose pupils were the children of the servants of the Empress of Russia. From these beginnings, the most famous school in the world, the Kirov School, developed. Soon there was another school, in Moscow, from which the Bolshoi Ballet was to develop.

Both are great schools, but there are differences. Kirov dancers are famous for their lightness of movement and their aristocratic style; the Bolshoi-trained dancers are best known for amazing feats of acrobatics. At both schools, emphasis is placed on exercising the back. Dancers learn to arch their backs when they leap to sensational effect. Both companies use a system of dance training laid down by Agrippina Vaganova, who taught until her death in 1951.

These ballet students (right) are learning the Russian way. After years of training at the Kirov, the Bolshoi, and at other schools all over the Soviet Union, the time will come when the students have their final Graduation Examination in Dance.

Pictured here (below) is a group of students at the school of the National Ballet of Canada with their teacher, Betty Oliphant. British-born, she first went to Canada in 1949, opening a school in Toronto. She is a believer in the great training traditions of the Russian ballet and sees to it that for several months each year, a guest teacher from the Soviet Union gives her pupils the benefit of those traditions.

Training Around the World

No nation can hope to have a great ballet company without a fine school in which to train its dancers. There are a number of excellent schools around the world, as well as those in Russia, but two merit special attention.

The first is the Royal Danish Ballet School in Copenhagen. Its fame is due to the Danish choreographer August Bournonville (1805-79). Entrants to the school still study according to his methods. But they also train along more modern lines laid down by the Danish dancer Harald Lander, who took over the school in 1932. Helped by the Russian teacher Vera Volkova, he restored the fame of both the school and the company. The methods of the choreographer Flemming Flindt, who became director in 1966, increased the international standing of Danish ballet.

The other famous European school is that of the Paris Opéra Ballet, founded in 1731. Though the teaching has changed over the years, it is based on centuries of tradition. It was modernized by the Russian dancer Serge Lifar, who took over the Opéra from 1929-45.

These are students of the famous Royal Danish School (right) in Copenhagen.

In very grand surroundings (below) are students of the Paris Opéra School. All over the world there are fine schools hard at work producing dancers for the future.

There are many schools in Germany. Nearly every opera house has a company attached to it. The finest of them all is the John Cranko School in Stuttgart. It was named after the British choreographer who, in the 1960s, made Stuttgart the dance capital of Germany. Other important dance groups are the Cologne Institute for Theater Dance and the Essen Folkwang School.

Italy's most famous classical ballet school belongs to the best known of all opera houses, La Scala, in Milan. Carla Fracci, the most famous Italian dancer of modern times, was trained there.

Today ballet flourishes throughout the world, and there are schools in places as far apart as China, Japan, and South America. Though methods may vary around the world, one thing is certain: Every course is based on very hard work over many years.

Making a Ballet

When the lights go down and the conductor steps into the orchestra pit, the music fills the theater, the curtain rises and the ballet begins. But it does not really start here at all. A ballet first takes shape in the mind of the choreographer. In deciding what his work will finally look like, the choreographer is ballet's equivalent of a Mozart, a van Gogh, a Shakespeare or any other great creative artist.

Although the dancers usually receive the loudest cheers, they would not do so if a beautiful ballet had not been created for them to dance. Without the choreographer there would be no ballet.

In this section of the book we look at the role of the key figure, the choreographer. The work he does involves many different skills. He invents the steps for the ballet and teaches them to the dancers. He must also make sure that the lighting, scenery and costumes are right and he is involved in a lot of the hard work behind the scenes.

Below is a delightful scene from the Royal Ballet's production of *Nutcracker*. Its choreographer was the great Russian dancer, Rudolf Nureyev.
It had its première at the Royal Opera House, in 1968.
Nureyev is now internationally famous as a choreographer.

Nureyev at Work

Choreographers think up ideas for ballets and decide which steps the dancers will use and how they will move on stage. They may use a story that is suitable for dance treatment, or decide to base a ballet on an idea, like hope or despair. They may want to create a ballet around a piece of music or, perhaps, to show off the talents of a particular dancer. Frederick Ashton often created ballets specially for Margot Fonteyn.

Choreographers first have to choose the music they want. Nowadays, because time is often short and the cost of commissioning a new music score is very high, they will probably use music already in existence. Once the music has been chosen rehearsals have to be arranged. The choreographer will come to the first rehearsal with the new ballet prepared in his mind.

Rudolf Nureyev first choreographed *Nutcracker* with the Royal Swedish Ballet in 1967, a year before his much-loved production for the Royal Ballet. The pictures on these pages show him working with his dancers on the ballet, which has many children in its cast as well as adult dancers. Like all choreographers, he is responsible for every aspect of the ballet. However, many people are there to assist him – including specialists like the designer and the conductor. Whether it is a totally original ballet, or a recreation of an old favorite, it is the choreographer on whom everything depends.

Nureyev is rehearsing (left and below) with that great star of the Royal Ballet, Merle Park. It was she who starred in the 1968 Royal Ballet production of the ballet at its premiere. These are glimpses of the exciting but strenuous backstage world that the public never sees.

The choreographer must be able to show his dancers what he wants them to do. He may just have a sketchy outline of what he wants, to start with, and he may not begin at the beginning of the ballet but choose some particular section on which to start working. He will always be an ex-dancer or a dancer, and his company will quickly grasp his ideas for steps and movements and also, sometimes, make suggestions. There is, however, no age limit for choreographers. Some of them are still hard at work in their 70s!

Choreographers

The choreographer, as well as rehearsing his dancers, will be working closely with the designer he has chosen to design the scenery and costumes. The job is a very skilled one. It is not enough to be a good painter. The scenery designs also have to work technically when they are built to stage size. The lighting designer has to make sure the stage and scenery are well-lit. There is also a costume designer. Unlike theatrical and operatic costumes, where clothes can be similar to what people actually wear or have worn, dance costumes must be designed for dancing. The costumes can suggest a period or nationality, but unrestricted movement is all-important for the dancers. And the costumes must be strong enough to endure constant contact with sweat, which rots material, for dancers perspire a lot because of their exertions under the hot lights.

The great Russian-born American choreographer George Balanchine (left) is rehearsing his own company, the New York City Ballet.

Frederick Ashton (below), like Balanchine, is a choreographer of genius whose career spans more than half a century. He is pictured here rehearsing Britain's first male superstar of international fame, Anthony Dowell.

Meanwhile, rehearsals are in progress most of the time, for the first night can be postponed only in exceptional circumstances. The choreographer cannot rehearse the dancers *all* the time, for most of them will be in other ballets, which they also need to practice.

Gradually, the dancers learn their steps and progress becomes more rapid, though a choreographer may take up a whole rehearsal to perfect a single important scene. There may still be drastic changes in the ballet at the last minute if the choreographer decides that a different approach will improve the work. Or a star dancer may be injured, and have to be replaced at the last minute.

Regardless of these last-minute changes, the ballet must be ready for the first night. The slightest flaw can ruin everything. That is why a dancer's life is so demanding, and the daily session at the barre can never be avoided. The dedication of the dancers and the choreographers who train them must be total.

The American-born choreographer Jerome Robbins (above) is rehearsing Mikhail Baryshnikov, who many regard as the greatest and most exciting male dancer of our age. Once a dancer, Robbins, as well as being a famous choreographer of ballets, has created dances for musicals and was chiefly responsible for that thrilling stage musical, *West Side Story*.

Twyla Tharp (right) also started as a dancer, and is now one of the most-talked-about choreographers of the day. Many of her ballets are slick and amusing. One of the most famous is *Push Comes To Shove*. She has her own company but choreographs for other companies as well.

The Benesh System

Until fairly recently, the steps of a ballet had to be learned and passed down from the original choreographer through ballet masters to new companies of dancers. Various ways of recording the steps of a whole ballet were tried, some being quite successful until, in 1947, Rudolf Benesh developed a system of "movement notation" that is now very widely used. Now a choreologist is present to write down the movements created by the choreographer when he or she rehearses the dancers.

On paper, there are five lines that represent the top of the dancer's head, the top of the shoulders, waist, knees, and floor. The signs for the position of the dancer's body are written above, on, or below these lines, so each position can be read.

An example of the Benesh system shown here (right) is the choreologist's version of the steps the dancers are performing in the picture below. Ballet stars and choreographers still hand down the steps of a ballet from memory, but now old and new ballets can be recorded, as music is in a score.
Rudolf Benesh's system of recording movement has proved one of the key developments in the long history of ballet. His wife, Joan, a former dancer, is teaching students (left).

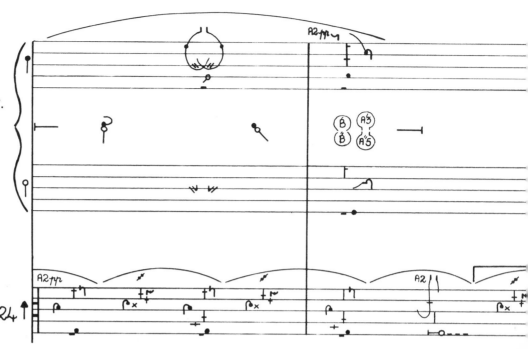

Staging a Ballet
The Theater

Ballets can be performed in all sorts of surroundings, but an opera house or theater provides the best setting, as they are specially geared to present this kind of work. There are designers, lighting directors, conductors, and musicians, and everyone backstage, all available to help. Of course, the dancers are important but they are part of a team, all of whom are vital if the performance of a new – or old – ballet is to go smoothly.

The audience will go to the opera house or theater confident that nothing will go wrong. It is miraculous that it scarcely ever does. Some theaters, usually modern ones, are well-equipped backstage, but many historic theaters are difficult to work in. The equipment may be old and out-moded and space may be limited. The beautiful Royal Opera House, Covent Garden, is shared by the Royal Opera and the Royal Ballet, who are assisted by an army of backstage staff. The audience sees the glamorous side of the theater, but behind the scenes there are a multitude of problems. The unseen technical staff is as important to the ballet as the dancers and choreographers.

Theaters and opera houses are the dancers' professional homes and performing arenas, where the choreographer's work is on display for audiences and critics alike. This is where a ballerina may be acclaimed in a role that, only a few days earlier, she thought she would never be able to master, as she despaired of achieving what her choreographer asked of her.

Once the curtain has gone up on a first night, the ballet is out of the hands of the choreographer. His ballet may entertain, thrill, sadden or cheer us, but in performance, it is up to his dancers to do their best and to the audience to respond in its own way. It is hardly surprising that a first night is particularly nerve-wracking for the choreographer.

London's Royal Opera House, Covent Garden, is one of the most beautiful theaters in the world. This is how Covent Garden looks when the audience is just starting to come in for the performance. Note the orchestra pit where you can see some of the players, and see if you can pick out a line of spotlights above the top row of boxes. There are many more facing the stage, which you cannot see, and, of course, still more at the front, the sides, and above the stage. Panels open up in the dome to allow strong spotlights to follow the stars.

Some of the people in the auditorium are reading their programs. These contain interesting facts about the ballet they are about to see, as well as its story, if it has one. There is also a list of the names of the dancers, director, producer, and backstage staff as well as the all-important choreographer. But now, on with the ballet!

Before the Performance

Long before the audience is let into the theater, there is activity backstage. Our pictures show that much-loved star of the Royal Ballet, Lesley Collier, getting ready for a performance of *Romeo and Juliet*. At the same time, dozens of other dancers are also arriving. From the moment they come into the theater through the stage door, they have only one object in mind: to be ready to give their all in the performance of the ballet.

Lesley Collier is British and was born in 1947. A pupil of the Royal Academy of Dancing and of the Royal Ballet School, she joined the company in 1965 and became a principal in 1972. We shall follow her through an evening at the ballet, and see life on the other side of the footlights.

Lesley Collier, beautiful star and principal of the Royal Ballet Company, arrives at the stage door and collects her mail from the stage-door keeper.

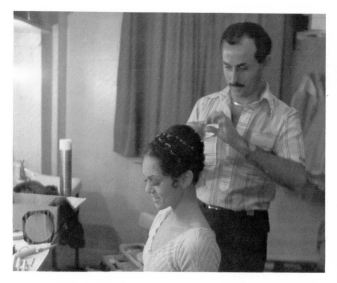

Naturally her hair and her makeup must be exactly right. She has a hairdresser to do her hair for each performance (above). Makeup, too, is a very skilled art (right), and it must look natural in all parts of the theater, especially under the harsh lights. Some dancers must put on heavy "character" makeup if they are playing, say, a witch.

She is dancing Juliet in *Romeo and Juliet* by Prokofiev tonight. Her partner is Mikhail Baryshnikov – a thrilling prospect for the packed audience.

There is much to be done before the curtain goes up on the ballet, and all of it is an important part of her performance. She must look and feel like Juliet.

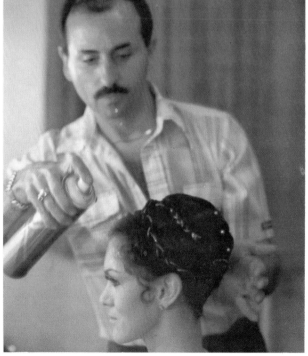

Now our star is almost ready to proceed to the next stage of preparation – warming up – for the performance that is so eagerly awaited.

Behind the Scenes

An opera house may appear to the audience to be a glamorous place. It seems orderly and ready for the performance. But backstage the atmosphere is lively and sometimes tense. The lack of space backstage in some old theaters makes working conditions difficult, and is in stark contrast to the conditions "front of house" where the audience sits.

There is always some tension behind the scenes as performers and technicians prepare themselves for the raising of the curtain, but everyone concerned with the performance is highly skilled. In the paint-shop the sets, built by expert carpenters to the designer's specifications, have been painted. The lighting designer's plans are put into operation by the chief electrician. His job is now easier than it once was.

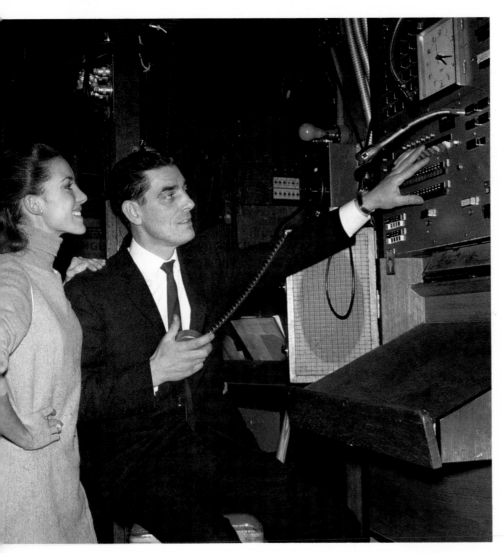

It is always an exciting moment when the musicians start filing into the orchestra pit (above). Then they tune up and, as the houselights fade, the conductor comes in. The music starts and the performance begins. On the left are two skilled technicians. They are in charge of the lighting and all its wonderful atmospheric effects. During an intermission (right), enthusiastic ballet fans have some refreshments and discuss the dancers and their performance.

These days, the lighting changes can be pre-set before a performance, and lighting effects are more amazing today than ever before.

There is likely to be a full orchestra in the orchestra pit, though some ballets only require small groups of musicians, or, in some cases, the music may be pre-recorded. When there is a conductor, he or she will be a specialist, because to accompany dancers on stage requires great musical expertise. If a new score has been written for the ballet, the musicians will have had extra rehearsals to get to know the piece.

The audience who sits watching the ballet and discussing it between the acts, may not know anything of this strange world backstage. What they should always be aware of, however, is the sheer hard work and the dedication that have gone into staging the ballet.

Warming Up

A dancer must warm up his or her muscles before a performance, just as a musician must tune his instrument. The dancers wear leg-warmers until the muscles are warmed, just as they do at the start of the daily class that all dancers attend. It is all part of the preparation for the strenuous work that will take place on stage. All that remains for the choreographer to do now, is to offer some final words of advice and wish his dancers luck. Backstage, all around the theater, people are ready to go into action when the curtain finally goes up.

There is tension in the air, the sort of tension that bears no relation to fright. The right amount of tension can improve the performance on stage and generate excitement in the audience as well. Then, the voice on the loudspeaker announces that there is a quarter of an hour to go before the curtain rises.

Lesley Collier was hard at work at the barre this morning. Now she is hard at work again warming up in preparation for the moment when she will make her first entrance as Juliet in *Romeo and Juliet*. The phrase "warm up" is used to describe a series of exercises that all ballet dancers must perform to loosen and relax their muscles. Lesley Collier and her colleagues will perform effortlessly on stage movements that are quite beyond the physical capabilities of ordinary people. But they cannot dance while their muscles are stiff, so the warming-up exercises are a crucial part of a ballet dancer's preparation.

Final Preparations

The audience fills the theater and the hum of voices gradually gets louder. Backstage, it is time for last-minute adjustments to costumes, the all-important ballet shoes are checked, and some movements are practiced. Some dancers may try to enjoy a moment of total relaxation before they go on stage. Suddenly, it is time for the performers to go to the side of the stage, or onto it, to await their cue. The orchestra can be heard tuning up in the pit. The noise from the audience is louder than ever. With seconds to go, the houselights dim.

A ballet dancer's shoes (below) may look delicate but, in fact, they have been carefully strengthened. The costume, too, though very attractive, must be strong enough to stand up to the strains that it will be subjected to.

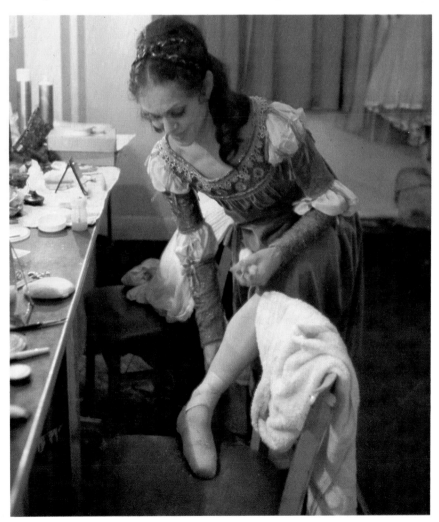

Curtain Up!

The curtain rises, and all the seemingly endless hard work that has gone on in preparation for this moment is brought to a climax. The ballet begins and, during the performance, the dancers, music, scenery, and costumes form a magic blend. The audience is important, too, for without one no form of theater can exist. In this production of *Romeo and Juliet* two great stars of the ballet, Lesley Collier and Mikhail Baryshnikov, dance the title roles at the Royal Opera House in Covent Garden.

Lesley Collier and Mikhail Baryshnikov, dancing the roles of Romeo and Juliet (above and right), the two most famous lovers in all theater.

Romeo finds Juliet's unconscious body. Believing her to be dead, he poisons himself. Juliet awakens, realizes what has happened, then she stabs herself. The two lovers lie dead (left).

The ballet *Romeo and Juliet* is about two ill-fated lovers. Their families, the Capulets and the Montagues, are bitter enemies. They meet at a masked ball and fall in love, but their relationship is doomed from the start. In the end, the couple both die and, too late, their families realize what they have done. It is a moving ballet that is based on Shakespeare's play of the same title. The beautiful and thrilling music is by the great Russian composer Serge Prokofiev. It is one of the finest scores ever written for a ballet. Several different choreographers have produced their versions of this ballet, and it has been performed all over the world.

Gerd Larsen (above) as Juliet's nurse, a role in which she was famous. Miss Larsen is a ballet teacher and an expert on mime.

Curtain Calls

The curtain falls on the last act of the ballet, and a mighty roar of cheers and thunderous applause erupts from the audience. The dancers acknowledge the applause and take the final curtain calls, bringing the evening to a magical close. *Romeo and Juliet*, with Collier and Baryshnikov dancing together, was a total success.

Sometimes the audience and critics do not receive new ballets so well. Whether the critics are right or wrong, it is the audiences, finally, who decide whether a ballet is successful. No company can continue to perform, night after night, without an audience.

Whatever happens to particular ballets, however, the dancers will be back at the barre or in the rehearsal room the next day. For them the work does not depend on a single performance, it never stops!

The performance is over and Lesley Collier (right) takes a bow. She has scored another triumph in her soaring career. Many in the audience (below) cannot imagine a more romantic Juliet.

The stars of the evening go home. Around the world other performances are coming to an end, and some lucky audiences may have glimpsed the magic of the art of ballet at its incomparable best.

Backstage

It is over! Gradually, the theater empties. Everyone seems to be smiling or talking excitedly, for the evening has been a triumph.

The critics are the first to leave. They will describe the performance in their newspapers. They may not all be of the same opinion, just as ordinary balletgoers often disagree, but the critics are historians of ballet who, if they are skilled, will encourage people to come and see a new work. They also leave a record of the ballet and its dancers for future generations.

Meanwhile, backstage, congratulations are being showered on the choreographer and his stars. He will have plenty on his mind, for he knows that, successful as the evening was, the ballet can still be improved. Some of his ideas may not have worked very well. Others may need altering.

The ballerina and her partner, too, excited as they are by the cheers and thrilling reception they have had, will be eager for the choreographer's opinion, for they are both far too dedicated to believe that they cannot achieve even more with his guidance. No one in the cast will sit on their laurels and believe themselves to be perfect. The greater the artist, the more he or she will strive to achieve perfection.

Visitors come around to see the stars, congratulate them, and thank them for the joy they have given. The atmosphere is relaxed and happy after the hard physical work that ballet demands. It is the most taxing of all the arts, though the strain must never show, just the amazing skill that onlookers find almost supernatural.

Finally, after changing, it is time to go home. Outside the stage door a crowd is waiting to cheer the stars as they leave. Some lucky fans may be able to snatch a word with them, get their autographs, or just gaze in wonder at the ballet dancers. For they have seen a marvelous performance and want to show their appreciation.

The choreographer, Kenneth MacMillan, talking to his stars after the performance (above).

With Lesley Collier looking on, Baryshnikov is congratulated by Dame Ninette de Valois, founder of the Royal Ballet (left). In the background is Kenneth MacMillan.

Outside the theater (right) the fans are waiting for the stars, autograph books at the ready. Soon the whole vast opera house will be closed for the night. Tomorrow another day of hard work begins.

49

The History of Ballet
First Ballets

Although people have always danced, the art we call ballet was born in Italy and France over 400 years ago. Magnificent performances staged in Italy combined dance, song, and spectacle. These spread over Europe and courtiers took part in them. In the mid-1600s, at the French court of Louis XIV, real ballets sprang from these entertainments and the king himself participated. The five positions were worked out, and French became the language of ballet because it was in France that the new art developed.

In the 18th century, Jean-Georges Noverre turned ballet into an art that combined dramatic dancing with a story. Yet ballet as we know it dates from the early 19th century, when the romantic movement started in all the arts, including ballet. Around 1820, female dancers went up on pointe for the first time, and this new form of virtuosity was used to suggest flight and supernatural beings.

Marie Taglioni (above), the queen of ballet's romantic era, was born in 1804. Her success in *La Sylphide* in 1832, five years after her debut, made her famous throughout Europe and changed ballet history. The Royal Danish Ballet still performs *La Sylphide* (right) in a version staged by August Bournonville in 1836.

Another great moment in early ballet history was the premiere of *Giselle* in Paris in 1841, with another star of the romantic era, Carlotta Grisi, in the title role. The work is one of the earliest ballets still performed regularly today. Nearly every great ballerina has danced the title role of the peasant girl who dies of love. Natalia Makarova and Mikhail Baryshnikov (left) dance *Giselle*.

Tchaikovsky's Ballets

In the second half of the 19th century the quality of ballet in Europe declined, and women often danced men's parts as well as their own. Only in Russia were standards of dancing maintained, especially by two Frenchmen, Arthur St. Léon, whose *Coppélia* is still very popular, and Marius Petipa. Petipa had the good luck to work with the composer Tchaikovsky, whose magnificent scores for *Swan Lake*, *The Sleeping Beauty*, and *Nutcracker* are masterpieces.

Strangely, *Swan Lake* was a failure when it was first performed in Moscow in 1877; until you consider that the first performance was arranged by a useless choreographer and an appalling conductor. Old scenery and costumes and a second-rate ballerina were used. Incredibly, a third of Tchaikovsky's music was removed to make way for fourth-rate music by someone else. Not until 1895, after Tchaikovsky's death, was the ballet re-choreographed by Petipa and Ivanov. It is now very popular.

Merle Park and Anthony Dowell (below) perform a ballet classic, *Swan Lake*. The story is about a prince called Siegfried who falls in love with a swan queen, Odette. Odette and her friends have been put under a spell by the wicked Rotbart. Only at midnight can the swans briefly return to their human form. Rotbart, hoping to separate the lovers, disguises his daughter Odile as Odette, and takes her to a ball where Siegfried promises to marry her, although he has promised to be faithful to Odette. Finally, the lovers are reunited.

The ballet *The Sleeping Beauty*, though not a failure at first like *Swan Lake*, got off to a mixed start as many people disliked the music. Fortunately, it was not a failure, and the role of Princess Aurora has been a supreme test for ballerinas ever since. The ballet is full of marvelous scenes, though it proves very costly to produce, and for many years a very shortened version was performed. All that has changed in recent years, and it is now performed in its entirety, to the delight of audiences everywhere.

Nutcracker was choreographed by Petipa's colleague, Ivanov. It was first performed in 1892 but it is not as well liked as *The Sleeping Beauty* or *Swan Lake*. But the music is beautiful and the ballet is a great favorite around the world, especially with young audiences. It is especially popular at Christmas. Little of Ivanov's original choreography survives today. Among the more recent productions is a very fine version by Rudolf Nureyev.

The many delights of *The Sleeping Beauty* include the marvelous dances and characters it contains – even cats (above). It was Petipa's greatest achievement and included many fine dances. The most famous of these is the Rose Adagio, when the Princess dances with each of her four suitors in turn and they all present her with two roses.

With *The Sleeping Beauty* Petipa's historic partnership with Tchaikovsky reached truly magnificent heights. Ballet may have been impoverished elsewhere, but in Russia, thanks mainly to these two men, it was flowering in the most remarkable way. Yet a new revolution in ballet was on the horizon. Not surprisingly, it was to break out in Russia.

Diaghilev

Despite the triumphs of Petipa and Tchaikovsky, even Russian ballet was unadventurous by 1900. Enter Serge Diaghilev! Born in Russia in 1872, he brought about a revolution in ballet that transformed it into the living, thrilling art we know today. He was a great organizer, not a dancer or choreographer, and he gathered a superb team around him that has never been equalled. They included perhaps the greatest of all choreographers, Mikhail Fokine; the artists, Bakst and Benois; composers of genius like Stravinsky; and legendary dancers, including Vaslav Nijinsky, Tamara Karsavina, and Anna Pavlova.

Fokine and Diaghilev wanted a total blend of dancing, music, painting, and acting and they achieved it. The company Diaghilev created was the Ballets Russes and it burst on Paris in 1909. The Polovstian Dances from *Prince Igor*, with music by Borodin, so thrilled the audience that it tore away the railing in front of the orchestra. When war began in 1914, the company stayed in the West. It was the most extraordinary assembly of talent in ballet history.

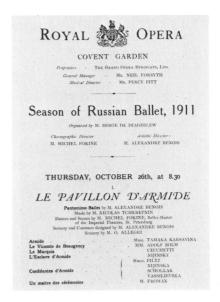

London was one of the fortunate capitals visited by the Diaghilev company (above).

Ann Jenner and Derek Rencher (below) in one of the Diaghilev ballets, *The Firebird*, choreographed by the great Fokine and with music by Igor Stravinsky. It was first performed in Paris in 1910 with Karsavina in the title role.

1 Anna Pavlova, a much-loved Diaghilev dancer, who later toured the world with her own company.
2 Tamara Karsavina in *Petrushka*, the colorful but tragic story of puppets brought to life.
3 Nijinsky and Karsavina in *The Specter of the Rose*. It was said of Nijinsky that he seemed to be able to pause at the top of his leaps.
4 An illustration of the folk tale *The Firebird*.

1

2

3

4

British Ballet

Two women did more than anyone else to bring ballet to Britain. They are Dame Ninette de Valois, born in Ireland in 1898, and Dame Marie Rambert, born in Poland in 1888. Both were dancers at a time when there was no such thing as British ballet, but they have changed all that. Marie Rambert, who had been with Diaghilev, started a school in London in 1920. This was the beginning of Ballet Rambert. Ninette de Valois teamed up with another amazing woman, Lilian Baylis, who in the 1920s was staging Shakespeare and opera cheaply at London's Old Vic Theatre. Ballet became part of the venture, and when Lilian Baylis reopened Sadler's Wells Theatre in 1931, the Vic-Wells (later Sadler's Wells) Ballet was born.

Early stars included Alicia Markova, Margot Fonteyn, Robert Helpmann, and the choreographer Frederick Ashton. Sadler's Wells Ballet moved to Covent Garden in 1946 and became "Royal" in 1956. Without those two women, British ballet would not be as famous as it is today.

Margot Fonteyn, the most acclaimed of all British dancers, is seen (above) in one of her most famous roles, the title part in *Ondine*. She joined the Vic-Wells Ballet in 1934 and her glorious career spanned 45 years.

A scene (left) from the London Festival Ballet's production of *Romeo and Juliet* by Nureyev.

A scene from *The Rake's Progress* (above), a ballet inspired by the famous paintings of William Hogarth. The choreographer was Ninette de Valois, in 1935.

Ballet Rambert's production of *Pierrot Lunaire* (right) with choreography by the American, Glen Tetley. Ballet Rambert, once a classical company, has now become a brilliant modern-dance group.

59

Russian Ballet

The Russian Revolution, which began in 1917, swept away a great deal, but ballet and the other arts survived. Diaghilev's magnificent company (see page 56) stayed in the West, but standards of dancing in Russia remained as high as ever, and they remain high today. Russian choreography, however, has been held back by state control. Too many modern Soviet ballets have strong, political messages and uplifting endings. Anything too modern has been frowned upon, which is the main reason why choreographers and dancers from Balanchine to Baryshnikov have left their homeland to seek artistic freedom elsewhere.

There are great companies all over the Soviet Union, but the two finest are still the stylish and aristocratic Kirov in Leningrad and the Bolshoi in Moscow, where vivid performances and amazing athleticism by the men are the rule. Both these great companies, and lesser ones, give memorable performances of the classics. The most famous modern Russian ballet is *Romeo and Juliet*, with Prokofiev's wonderful music. First performed in Czechoslovakia in 1938, it had its Russian premiere at the Kirov in 1940. The choreographer was Leonid Lavrovsky and the stars, Galina Ulanova and Konstantin Sergeyev. Alas, there are few modern Russian ballets to match the classical ballets.

An electrifying scene from *Spartacus* (right), which features the brilliant Maris Liepa as the villainous Roman commander Crassus, who puts down the revolt of gladiators and slaves led by Spartacus. The ballet, in which Good confronts Evil, Heroism faces Villainy, is too straightforward for some tastes, but scenes like this and many more have great theatrical impact.

The ballet *Raymonda* has been very popular in Russia ever since its first production in 1898. The choreographer was Marius Petipa. It is a large-scale work that needs a major company to do it justice. It is performed here (below left) by the great Kirov company of Leningrad.

A scene from *The Land of Miracles* (left), an exciting ballet in the repertoire of the Kirov. Pictured here are Soloviev as the Eagle and Sapogov as the King of the Monsters. The ballet was first produced in 1967 with choreography by Leonid Jacobson.

American Ballet

Ballet is more popular in America than ever before, thanks to a handful of extraordinary figures, the most important of whom was George Balanchine. Born in Russia in 1904, he left because his ideas were too advanced for the authorities. After working in Europe, he came to the United States in 1934, and he and Lincoln Kirstein founded the School of American Ballet. In 1948 they established the New York City Ballet. Over the years, Balanchine choreographed more than 150 ballets for the company. His friendship with his fellow Russian, Igor Stravinsky, resulted in many masterpieces. Balanchine has done more for ballet in the United States than any other person.

America's other great company is the American Ballet Theatre, founded in 1939. It concentrates on star performances. Its artists included Makarova and the company's new artistic director, Baryshnikov. Jerome Robbins, who has also worked with Balanchine, and Agnes de Mille are two choreographers who worked with the ABT.

America's first all-black classical company, the Dance Theater of Harlem, in *Troy Game* (above).

Merrill Ashley in the New York City Ballet's production of *Square Dance* (left), with choreography by the company's ballet master, George Balanchine. A scene from American Ballet Theatre's production of *Giselle* (right). The lovers are Mikhail Baryshnikov and Gelsey Kirkland in this happy moment from act one of the ever-popular romantic masterpiece.

World Ballet

Ballet began in the courts of Italy and France, but now spans the world. Since the end of World War II in 1945, companies have been formed even in countries where there had been no tradition of ballet.

Such was the case in Japan, whose finest group, the Tokyo Ballet Company, was founded in 1960 as a school. It was transformed in 1964 by Koichi Hyashi, who brought in experts from Moscow's Bolshoi to start the young company off with the highest standards.

Ballet in Australia dates back to the 1830s, and many famous stars visited the country through the years, including Anna Pavlova, that roving ambassadress for ballet. But native Australian ballet can be said to date from 1942, when a Czech dancer, Edouard Borovansky, founded a company in Melbourne, which, in 1962, became the now internationally famous Australian Ballet. This exciting young company tours extensively and is well received wherever it goes.

Its first director was the Royal Ballet's Peggy van Praagh, and later directors have been the great Australian dancer and actor, Sir Robert Helpmann, and, from 1976, Anne Woolliams. She is a British teacher who had a distinguished career at Stuttgart and elsewhere. Then the ballerina Marilyn Rowe took over. Famous visiting choreographers have included the Americans, Glen Tetley and John Butler, also Nureyev (whose *Don Quixote* for the company is world famous), and George Balanchine and Frederick Ashton. Most Australian states have their own companies and modern-dance groups.

Canada's finest company is the National Ballet of Canada, founded by the British dancer Celia Franca in 1951. She directed it until 1974. An ex-Sadler's Wells and Ballet Rambert star, she based it on British lines. Canada's two other leading companies are the Royal Winnipeg Ballet, founded in 1939, and Les Grands Ballets Canadiens of Montreal. When not performing in their home towns, these Canadian companies often visit the United States.

A colorful scene from the Australian Ballet's production of *Petrushka* (above), a work in the repertoire of companies all over the world.

A scene from a ballet performed by the Asami Maki Classical Ballet of Tokyo (right). The name of the ballet is *Kakubei-Jishi* and the dancers are Yoko Shimizu as the Girl and Toshihiko Fujiki as the Boy. Japan has a tradition of dancing that goes back for many centuries. Recently they have moved into modern ballets. However, the Japanese are also great lovers of Western ballet.

A scene from the National Ballet of Canada's production of *Don Juan* (left), with choreography by John Neumeier. It is an individual approach to the story of the Spanish lover, who has appeared in plays, other ballets, and in Mozart's opera, *Don Giovanni*. This is one of the many dramatic scenes in the ballet. The leading role of Don Juan has often been danced by Rudolf Nureyev, who has appeared with the company as a guest on a number of occasions.

65

European Experiments

Ballet lovers look forward to new experiences, unlike many music and opera lovers, who tend to be more traditional. This means that the choreographers can experiment. Today's most famous experimenter is French-born Maurice Béjart, founder of the Ballet of the 20th Century, which is based in Brussels, Belgium, but tours widely. Its theatrical impact is terrific, and Béjart is so keen to appeal to a vast public of all ages that his ballets are performed in tents and sports arenas as well as in theaters. He uses classical music, rock music, and whatever else he feels will emphasize his point. Although critics gnash their teeth at his simple methods, the public loves him!

Meanwhile, in Holland, more artistic modern ballet is danced by the Netherlands Dance Theater, which was formed in 1959, when a group broke away from the Dutch National Ballet. Combining classical and modern ideas, and with brilliant choreographers – Hans van Manen, Jaap Flier, Glen Tetley.

The Royal Danish Ballet is adventurous as well. Without abandoning its long classical tradition of Bournonville ballets, this company also presents modern works. The company's key figure from 1965 to 1978 was Flemming Flindt. The director is now Henning Kronstam. The Royal Danish often visits the United States and is always well received.

Rudolf Nureyev and Natalia Makarova (above) in one of the most famous European ballets of our time, Flemming Flindt's *The Lesson*. This Danish choreographer first choreographed the ballet for television in 1963. He then staged it for the Opéra Comique. It is about a teacher who is so carried away by what he teaches that he kills his pupil. It is based on a play by the playwright Eugène Ionesco.

A scene from *Nijinsky, Clown of God* (left), which the French-born choreographer Maurice Béjart created for his Ballet of the 20th Century. It is a vivid tribute to the legendary Russian dancer, Nijinsky, who is seen in some of his most famous roles.

A scene danced by the Netherlands Dance Theater (right).

Modern Dance

The modern-dance movement, which first set out to be anti-ballet, now plays an important role in expanding the future of the art of dance. The pioneer of modern dance was Isadora Duncan, who had next to no ballet training, but who hoped to recapture the freedom of the dances of ancient Greece. She was born in San Francisco in 1878 and she

The legendary pioneer of modern dance, Isadora Duncan (above).

toured widely giving dance recitals in Europe and Russia as well as in the United States. Her ideas caused a genuine stir.

Another American, Martha Graham, born in 1898, had real ballet training, but her ideas were even more startling than Duncan's. Still very active today as a choreographer, Martha Graham built up a wonderful company to perform her "dance plays." At first there was an enormous gulf between the Graham company and classical ballet, but this is no longer true today. Though classically trained dancers can switch to modern dance, modern dancers cannot switch to the classics. Classical dancers must undergo years of rigorous training to achieve their special "turned out" technique.

Ballet Rambert's production of *The Tempest* (left), a ballet inspired by Shakespeare's play set on a mysterious island.

The Martha Graham Dance Company broke new ground in 1979 when film star and entertainer Liza Minnelli joined the company for *The Owl and the Pussycat* (right). This was a modern-dance version of Edward Lear's poem of that name and Minnelli was the Storyteller.

Martha Graham (bottom right) has created more than 150 works. This is her solo, *Imperial Gesture* (1935).

68

There are two notable British modern-dance companies. The London Contemporary Dance Theatre was founded in 1967 and is closely connected with the Martha Graham company, as its artistic director, Robert Cohan, is an ex-member. However, the LCDT's ideas are its own.

The other British modern-dance company is Ballet Rambert, which was founded as a classical troupe (see pages 58-59). However, the classics were too expensive to stage so it turned to modern dance. It has a fine group of solo dancers.

Stars of Today

Baryshnikov and Makarova! They are the most exciting and many would say, the greatest dancers in the world today. Both were stars of Leningrad's Kirov Ballet, but they now work solely in the West. Mikhail Baryshnikov was born in 1948. He seems able to defy the laws of gravity. He joined the American Ballet Theatre after defecting to the West, but left that company to work with Balanchine at the New York City Ballet. Baryshnikov returned to the ABT as its director in 1980; nevertheless, he continues to perform.

Natalia Makarova, born in 1940, has partnered Baryshnikov on many occasions for the American Ballet Theatre and elsewhere. Her technique, personality, and acting ability make her supreme in classical and modern roles.

The incomparable Natalia Makarova (right) as Odette in *Swan Lake*, one of her many great roles. She and Baryshnikov, both of them Kirov-trained, sometimes perform together, occasions that every member of the audience will remember.

A dazzling leap (below) by Mikhail – nicknamed "Misha" – Baryshnikov, ballet's most exciting male dancer, whose brilliance is hailed whenever he performs.

Eva Evdokimova, born in Switzerland in 1948, was trained in Germany, England, Denmark and, finally, at the incomparable Kirov School in Leningrad. Though famous for her modern roles, she has achieved her greatest successes in the classics. In roles like La Sylphide and Giselle, her lyrical style, beauty, and amazing lightness of movement have made her a favorite with audiences. She performs as a guest artist with many of the leading ballet companies.

It was a tremendous stroke of luck when Rudolf Nureyev settled in the West. He was born in Russia in 1938, and was trained at the Kirov. His long partnership with Margot Fonteyn at the Royal Ballet is part of ballet legend. Since the mid-1960s he has become a major choreographer and remains one of the greatest male dancers of all time.

Rudolf Nureyev (below) has that rare quality of being able to create excitement every time he appears on stage, even before he begins to dance. He combines natural ability, Kirov training, and personal magnetism.

Eva Evdokimova (left) dancing Odette in *Swan Lake* with the London Festival Ballet. She became a prima ballerina when she was in her early 20s. For many ballet lovers she conjures up the lost world of the magical era of romantic ballet. Her Aurora in *The Sleeping Beauty* is as enchanting as her Odette-Odile in *Swan Lake*.

Talent abounds on these two pages, which feature three superstars of ballet. The magnificent Danish dancer-choreographer Peter Schaufuss, whose parents were both dancers, was born in 1949 and trained at the great Royal Danish School. He has appeared with many companies, and has been a principal dancer with the New York City Ballet, the National Ballet of Canada, and the London Festival Ballet. He is destined to be one of the great figures in ballet.

On the right are Merle Park and Anthony Dowell in *Swan Lake*. Merle Park joined the Royal Ballet in 1954. Famed for her technical skill and brilliant acting, she has danced a vast range of roles in her years with the company.

Anthony Dowell is one of the most exciting male dancers in the world. Born in Great Britain in 1943, he is renowned as a *danseur noble*, a superb technician who can play princes and other aristocratic roles as though to the manner born. After a long partnership with Antoinette Sibley, he has now begun a much acclaimed partnership with Natalia Makarova and dances on both sides of the Atlantic. For several years he was a leading dancer of the American Ballet Theatre.

Peter Schaufuss (above) as James in his much acclaimed production of *La Sylphide* for the London Festival Ballet. The ballet was staged to commemorate the 100th anniversary of the choreographer August Bournonville. Schaufuss was a pupil at the famous Danish school and later a star of the company.

Merle Park and Anthony Dowell (right) as Odette and Prince Siegfried in the most loved of all ballets, Tchaikovsky's *Swan Lake*. That it was a failure when it was first produced in 1877 will always astonish its millions of admirers. Merle Park is a magnificent Odette-Odile, while Anthony Dowell's wonderful qualities as a *danseur noble* are always in evidence when he dances.

Nadezhda Pavlova is no relation to the immortal Anna Pavlova, who died half a century ago, but she is one of Russia's stars in her own right. She was born at Tsheboksari in Russia in 1956, and studied not at the Kirov or the Bolshoi schools, but at Perm in the Ural Mountains, which has a long tradition of ballet dating back to 1821. During World War II, the Kirov Ballet was evacuated there, which gave local ballet a boost.

The young Pavlova graduated in 1974, having already, in 1973, won the All-Soviet Ballet Competition in Moscow, and the Grand Prix of the International Ballet Competition, also held in Moscow, two giant steps on the ladder of fame. Clearly, she was destined for stardom and she became a member of the Bolshoi in 1975. She is married to a very fine dancer, Vatcheslav Gordeyev, another star of the Bolshoi.

In 1976, she appeared in the *The Blue Bird*, the American film made in Russia. Ballet lovers in Russia eagerly wait to see what she will be offering them in the 1980s.

The galaxy of dancers on these pages represents Moscow's world-famous Bolshoi Ballet at its finest. Criticisms are made of modern Russian choreography, which is unadventurous and has led to a number of dancers leaving the great companies for the West. But there has never been serious criticism of Russian dancers, who rank as the most gifted and technically accomplished artists in the world.

The magnificent Nadezhda Pavlova (below), one of the Bolshoi's brightest stars.

Natalia Bessmertnova (right) as Kitri in the Bolshoi Ballet's production of *Don Quixote*.

A typically spectacular moment from the electrifying ballet *Spartacus* (below), one of the most exciting dance spectacles ever created at the Bolshoi or anywhere else. Vladimir Vasiliev is holding his wife, Yekaterina Maximova, in a striking pose. Many critics find fault with *Spartacus* for its rather conventional choreography and over-simple message, but it is theatrically so effective that audiences usually go wild with excitement.

Natalia Bessmertnova is another Bolshoi star. She is a famous dancer in the classical repertory, who was born in 1941 and joined the Bolshoi company 20 years later. She has also danced many modern roles, including Phrygia in *Spartacus* and Juliet in *Romeo and Juliet*. She performs frequently with her husband, the famous dancer-choreographer, Yuri Grigorovich. She is a performer of great charm, and, like Nadezhda Pavlova, she is very popular in Russia.

One of ballet's greatest and most loved husband-and-wife partnerships is that of Vladimir Vasiliev and Yekaterina Maximova. Vasiliev is a truly heroic dancer, tremendously athletic even by Russian standards, while Maximova, with whom he often dances, has been greatly loved ever since her debut at the Bolshoi in 1958. The couple has triumphed with the company not only at home, but on tour. Vasiliev was born in 1940 and Maximova in 1939.

Both dancers have created a number of leading roles in Soviet ballets and Vasiliev has become a choreographer. He won the much-coveted Nijinsky prize in Paris in 1964, and he and his wife have appeared in films and on television.

Ballet is becoming more and more popular in the United States, and the two stars pictured here, Peter Martins and Suzanne Farrell of the New York City Ballet, are great favorites with audiences in America and elsewhere.

Suzanne Farrell was born in Cincinnati in 1945. She joined the company in 1961 and became a soloist four years later. She excels in ballets by the company's legendary director and choreographer, the late George Balanchine, creating many roles for him. Then, in 1970, she went to Europe to join Maurice Béjart's Ballet of the 20th Century, which is based in Brussels, Belgium.

In Belgium, Suzanne Farrell created new roles, including one in the famous ballet, *Nijinsky, Clown of God*, but she returned to the United States and the New York City Ballet in 1975, internationally known because of her work with the always controversial Béjart. She has created roles in ballets by Balanchine and Jerome Robbins. She is one of the finest American-born dancers.

Peter Martins, born in Denmark in 1946, attended the Royal Danish Ballet School in Copenhagen. He became a member of the school's parent company, the Royal Danish Ballet, in 1965, becoming a soloist two years later. Then, in 1969, he came to the United States to become a principal dancer of the New York City Ballet. When Balanchine died in 1983, Martins was named artistic director.

Peter Martins had danced with other companies, including the London Festival Ballet, as a guest artist. He and Suzanne Farrell both created roles in Jerome Robbins's ballet, *Piano Concerto in G* (1975). They belong to a company which, some say, frowns on stars and concentrates on choreography. But wonderful dancers like Farrell and Martins are stars that cannot be hidden.

Peter Martins, the Danish-born dancer with American-born Suzanne Farrell (right) in the New York City Ballet's production of *Symphony in C*. Choreography is by George Balanchine and music by Georges Bizet. The ballet was first performed as long ago as 1947.

Two Canadian and two British stars are pictured on these pages: Karen Kain and Frank Augustyn of the National Ballet of Canada; and David Wall and Alfreda Thorogood of the Royal Ballet.

David Wall became the youngest principal in the history of the Royal Ballet in 1966, when he was only 20. Strong and handsome, he has danced in all the great classical ballets, and has created many modern roles including Prince Rudolf in *Mayerling*. He is married to the striking and beautiful Alfreda Thorogood, and they have often danced together. She joined the Royal Ballet at Covent Garden in 1970 and retired in 1980.

Karen Kain, born in 1951, joined Canada's leading company in 1969, becoming a principal two years later. She has often partnered Nureyev in the company and has danced with many foreign companies. Frank Augustyn, who was born in 1953, joined the Canadian company in 1970 and became a principal three years later.

Karen Kain and Frank Augustyn (above) in *Collective Symphony*, a ballet staged by the National Ballet of Canada, with choreography by the Dutch dancer-choreographer Hans van Manen. Both these very popular dancers were born in Canada.

David Wall (right) pictured here with Alfreda Thorogood, has often partnered Margot Fonteyn, who now belongs to history and legend. He has danced on four continents. Thorogood has danced all the great classical roles, and in many modern ballets.

Wayne Sleep (above) taking to the air in his usual dramatic fashion in the ballet *Cinderella*. He has acted in Shakespeare, pantomime, and a musical.

David Wall and Lesley Collier in *Swan Lake* (right) are both stars in the world of ballet. They have both starred in many new productions.

Pictured on these pages are just some of the dancers who help maintain the international fame of Britain's Royal Ballet. Wayne Sleep has been a soloist with the company since 1970, and he has also worked as a stage, film, and television actor. He is a genuine character dancer, small and tremendously agile, with a fine sense of comedy.

Lesley Collier (see pages 38-49) and David Wall are both stars of the Royal Ballet. Born in 1946, David Wall joined the Royal Ballet in 1963. His powerful personality and physique make him a striking hero in the classical roles, and he has created many roles in modern ballets, including the villain, Lescaut, in *Manon*.

Much of Rudolf Nureyev's career (see page 73) was with the Royal Ballet, where he was permanent guest artist for many years. His partner in the picture is Canadian-born Jennifer Penney, who comes from Vancouver and joined the Royal Ballet in 1963. She became a principal dancer in 1970. Nureyev is one of the world's most tireless dancers. He has appeared with the world's major ballet companies, as both star dancer and choreographer. A perfectionist, he demands the best and his fellow artists give their utmost.

As well as being a great artist, Rudolf Nureyev is one of those rare performers who raises the theatrical temperature every time he appears on stage. There are only a very few dancers, actors, and singers who have the personality and power to do this. They can actually project a sense of danger across the footlights! This sense of danger contributes to the excitement and involvement that an audience feels when watching a performance.

Stephen Jefferies is pictured in *Papillon*, a delightful ballet with music by Offenbach. He joined the Royal Ballet in 1969 and became a principal dancer in 1973. Stephen Jefferies has created a number of roles. He is married to the ex-dancer Rashna Homji.

Jennifer Penney and Rudolf Nureyev (above) in the ballet *Afternoon of a Faun*, set to Debussy's much-loved music.

Stephen Jefferies (below) in *Papillon*.

Ballet has become steadily more popular in Germany over the last 30 years, though Germany is not yet a leading dance nation. However, the city of Stuttgart has always had a tradition of ballet, and in 1960, with the arrival of choreographer John Cranko from Britain's Royal Ballet, the Stuttgart Ballet soared to fame. When Cranko died in 1973, the city's position in the ballet world was secure.

Cranko's leading ballerina, Marcia Haydée, became artistic director of the company in 1976. Her most famous roles include Juliet in *Romeo and Juliet* and Katharina (Kate) in *The Taming of the Shrew*; both ballets are based on Shakespeare's plays. She often dances with Richard Cragun. Two of their colleagues were Birgit Keil; and Egon Madsen, now in Munich.

Marcia Haydée, unlike some ballerinas, is a magnificent actress as well as a wonderful dancer. This means that in ballets with strong dramatic stories she gives performances of extraordinary dramatic interpretation. She was born in Brazil in 1939. The brilliant and powerful Cragun was born in Sacramento, California, in 1944.

Marcia Haydée and Richard Cragun (above) in John Cranko's ballet *The Taming of the Shrew*, inspired by Shakespeare's play. It was first performed by the Stuttgart Ballet in 1969 with these two great artists in the leading roles.

A colorful scene from *Coq d'Or* (right) with the Swiss dancer Manola Asensio as the Golden Cockerel. Originally it was an opera by the Russian composer Rimsky-Korsakov but in recent years, it has enjoyed great popularity as a ballet.

84

Manola Asensio was born in Switzerland in 1946. She studied at the famous school of ballet attached to La Scala Opera House in Milan, then she returned to her native country to dance with the Geneva Ballet. This was in the 1960s, when she was also performing with the Dutch National Ballet, the New York City Ballet, and the Harkness Ballet, also based in New York.

When the Harkness was disbanded in 1974, she became a principal dancer with the London Festival Ballet, with whom she still dances. She is seen below as the Golden Cockerel in *Coq d'Or*, with music by Rimsky-Korsakov. It was first performed by the Diaghilev Company in 1914. The London Festival Ballet staged it in 1974.

Jonas Kage is a Swedish dancer, born in 1950. After several years with the Royal Swedish Ballet, he joined the American Ballet Theatre in 1971 and soon became a principal dancer. He has since danced with the Stuttgart and with the Geneva Ballet, and the London Festival Ballet.

The Swedish dancer Jonas Kage (above) in the London Festival Ballet's production of *Sphinx*. Kage's international career has taken him to many countries, including Germany, Switzerland, and the United States.

New York is a ballet-lover's paradise, with great companies and great stars. Some of the stars are shown here.

Gelsey Kirkland was born in Pennsylvania in 1953. Trained at the School of American Ballet, she joined the New York City Ballet in 1968 and was soon dancing leading roles for the master choreographer, Balanchine. In 1974, she joined the American Ballet Theatre, and began dancing opposite the Russian superstars, Nureyev and Baryshnikov. Nureyev says of her that her movements are beautifully fluid and that she has "incredible strength for such a small girl." Baryshnikov, meanwhile, says that she improves from performance to performance. Praise indeed from such famous partners.

She reached a new peak in her career with her fiery rendering of Kitri in *Don Quixote* in 1978, a production that Baryshnikov choreographed. She tends to overwork, and at one time in her wonderful career she actually became too weak to perform. Fortunately, those days are over, and she is now one of the world's most exciting dancers. Her career goes from strength to strength and her every performance is eagerly awaited by her countless fans.

Gelsey Kirkland (left), one of the major stars of the ABT, is seen here as Giselle, a role that suits her dramatic talents.

Virginia Johnson (above), the magnificent black dancer of the Dance Theater of Harlem, is pictured performing in the ballet *Serenade*.

Merrill Ashley and Sean Lavery (right) perform *Square Dance*.

Virginia Johnson is one of our country's finest classical dancers. She is strong, has a superb technique, and is a star of the Dance Theater of Harlem, America's first classical company, which has only black dancers. It was founded as a school in 1968 by Arthur Mitchell and Karel Shook, and made its debut as a company three years later.

Merrill Ashley and Sean Lavery are two dancers from the New York City Ballet. These two stars are shown dancing in *Square Dance* by the director of their company, the late George Balanchine. The work was originally produced in New York in 1957.

The appeal of ballet is universal, so it is hardly surprising that more and more countries are producing fine ballet dancers. Ballet is certainly booming in Japan, and you can see two leading Japanese dancers performing in Tchaikovsky's *The Sleeping Beauty*. They are Tetsutaro Shimizv as Florimund and Yoko Morishita as the Princess Aurora. Yoko Morishita has been the prima ballerina of the Matsuyama Ballet Company since 1971, and has appeared as a guest star with the American Ballet Theatre and other leading companies. She made her debut, aged only 16, as Odette-Odile in *Swan Lake*.

Jorge Donn is a superb dancer from Argentina. He is now a star of Maurice Béjart's Ballet of the 20th Century. He is a powerful dancer with a commanding, exciting personality who has become internationally famous.

Tetsutaro Shimizv and Yoko Morishita (above), two of Japan's leading young dancers, in *The Sleeping Beauty*.

Jorge Donn (right) is seen here in Maurice Béjart's much-discussed ballet, *Nijinsky, Clown of God*, a study of the life of the most famous of all male ballet dancers, although it is not told in narrative sequence. Powerful and commanding, Donn is one of the most exciting talents to appear on the ballet scene in the late 1970s.

Ann Jenner is one of many British dancers who have first made their names in their home country, then left to star abroad. Born near London in 1944, she joined the Royal Ballet in 1961, becoming a principal in 1970. Now she has made an even greater name with the Australian Ballet.

Alexandra Radius and Han Ebbelaar are two very famous Dutch dancers and principals of the Dutch National Ballet. They are husband and wife, and have both also been members of the Netherlands Dance Theater and the American Ballet Theatre.

Elaine McDonald has starred in many roles for the Scottish Ballet. She was principal dancer of the Western Theatre Ballet, which became the Scottish Ballet in 1974.

An exciting glimpse of Ann Jenner (above) as the Firebird in the ballet of that name, one of the most striking roles in the repertoire of a ballerina.

Han Ebbelaar and his wife, Alexandra Radius (below), in Hans van Manen's ballet *Adagio Hammerklavier*, with music by Beethoven.

Elaine McDonald (right) as the heroine of *La Sylphide*. She is the Scottish Ballet's leading ballerina, and the ballet has a Scottish setting.

Two famous ballerinas star in this final selection of super-stars of the world of ballet. Galina Samsova was born in Russia in 1937. She joined the Kiev Ballet, where she met and married a Canadian, Alexander Ursuliak, and together they went to the National Ballet of Canada. From 1964-73, she was the ballerina of the London Festival Ballet, after which she and her second husband, André Prokovsky, created the New London Ballet. The company failed, but she is as busy as ever.

Margaret Barbieri is a star of the Sadler's Wells Royal Ballet. She joined the company in 1965 and became a principal in 1970. She dances the role of Lise in *La Fille mal gardée*. Frederick Ashton choreographed a sparkling new production of *La Fille mal gardée* for the Royal Ballet in 1960. Merle Park, one of the Royal Ballet's most acclaimed stars, was the second ballerina to dance the role of Lise. The first ballerina ever to dance the role of Lise in the ballet was Nadia Nerina.

Russian-born Galina Samsova (top left) in a striking pose, in *Paquita*, which she staged for the Sadler's Wells Royal Ballet. She has created many roles with the London Festival Ballet and other leading companies.

Despite her Italian-sounding name, Margaret Barbieri (above) was born in South Africa. Now a most popular British ballerina, she is seen here dancing in *Papillon*, a ballet with music by the operetta king, Jacques Offenbach.

Barbieri (right) in *La Fille mal gardée*. Her range is very wide indeed, and she excels in both classical and modern roles.

Glossary

ADAGIO A slow dance movement or series of exercises aimed at improving balance and line. It is also a section of the classical pas de deux where a ballerina displays her skill and line supported by her partner.

ARABESQUE In this pose one leg is extended behind the body, with the knee kept straight. The arms are placed in graceful positions. There are many different forms of the arabesque.

ATTITUDE This is a beautiful position, based on a statue of the god Mercury by Giovanni da Bologna. The body is supported on one leg, the other leg is raised in front or behind the body, and the knee is bent and turned outward. The arm on the same side of the body as the raised leg is above the head, while the other arm is held sideways.

BALLERINA The female dancer who performs the leading classical roles with a company. Some people wrongly use the word to describe any ballet dancer.

BALLET MASTER/BALLET MISTRESS He (or she) is in charge of the training of a company's dancers, and also of the rehearsals for the ballets that are being performed. He must keep the standard of a ballet high after the choreographer has completed his work. He also helps dancers make the most of their roles. The French name for a ballet master is "Maître de ballet."

BALLETOMANE A word used to describe those suffering from ballet-mania.

BALON The springiness or bounciness of a dancer's feet.

BARRE The wooden bar to be found along every ballet-class wall. Dancers use it for a variety of exercises at the beginning of their regular practice.

BATTERIE This describes a series of dance movements in which the feet are beaten together.

BOURREE A series of tiny steps that make the dancer seem to glide over the stage.

CHOREOGRAPHER The person who designs the ballet and decides which steps and movements the dancers will use and how they will move on stage.

CHOREOLOGIST The person who writes down the dancers' movements and steps.

CORPS DE BALLET Those members of a company who normally dance as a group.

DANCEUR NOBLE A male dancer who possesses a noble classical style.

DÉBUT A dancer's first appearance on stage.

DÉCOR A ballet's scenery. The same designer usually does costumes as well as scenery.

DIVERTISSEMENT A series of showpiece dances that have very little or no relation to the story of a ballet. The word is also used to describe a ballet without a story or mood.

ELEVATION The ability of a dancer to leap in the air.

ENCHAINEMENT A sequence of linked steps that become a continuous movement.

ENTRECHAT A jump during which the feet of a dancer criss-cross up to eight times in the air. The legendary Russian dancer Nijinsky is reputed to have achieved an entrechat ten times.

FOUETTÉ A step in which the dancer is on one leg and uses the other leg in a sort of whipping movement to help the body turn. This is performed, nearly always, by a female dancer on pointe. The most famous series of fouettés occur in the Black Swan pas de deux in *Swan Lake*. The ballerina has to execute 32 turns.

GLISSADE A sliding step.

JETÉ A leap from one foot to another. During the jump the foot on which the dancer is to land is kicked sideways, forward or backward.

LINE A very important feature of ballet. It refers to the "look" of the body when the dancer is dancing or just standing still. It is partly a matter of training, but the dancer must have an excellent physique in the first place.

94

MIME Acting without words. Ballet dancers must be able to express emotions through the use of mime.

MOVEMENTS There are seven basic movements which have to be learnt:
Plier (to bend)
Etendre (to stretch)
Relever (to rise)
Sauter (to jump)
Elancer (to dart)
Glisser (to glide)
Tourner (to turn)

PAS DE DEUX A dance for two dancers. *Pas* means step in French, so a *pas de quatre* means a dance for four, and so on.

PIROUETTE A turn on one leg, the dancer spins round on one foot.

PLIÉ A bend of the leg. Pliés are performed at the start of every dance class. They warm the muscles and are at the beginning and end of every leap.

POINTE The tip of the toe. It was early in the 19th century that the female dancers first danced on pointe, though until ballet shoes were strengthened later in the century, it was used only for momentary poses.

PORT DE BRAS This means the carriage of the arms and also refers to exercises that ensure that dancers' arms can be seen to their very best advantage.

POSITIONS There are five basic positions of the feet and arms that all ballet dancers have to learn.

PREMIERE The first performance of a ballet or play.

PRIMA BALLERINA A company's leading female dancer. Just a few ballerinas achieve the rare status of Prima Ballerina Assoluta. It is a rare honor. Only two Russian dancers earned the title over a 200-year period. Margot Fonteyn is the only British dancer to hold the title.

PRINCIPAL DANCER A leading dancer who dances the star roles for a company.

REHEARSAL Preparation of a ballet by the dancers before a performance.

REPERTORY The different ballets presented by a company over a period or a whole season.

SOLOIST A dancer who performs alone.

TERRE À TERRE It means ground to ground, and refers in ballet to a dance with few jumps.

TOMBE The dancer falls from one leg to the other or from both feet to one, bending the knee at the moment of landing.

TOUR EN L'AIR A turn – or two or three turns – in the air, usually only executed by male dancers – with tremendous effect.

TROUPE A company of dancers.

TUTU The famous ballet skirt – made of nylon or silk. It dates back to the early 19th century and Marie Taglioni, but in those days it was half way between the knee and the ankle.

WORKING LEG The dancer's leg that actually performs a movement, while the supporting leg is taking the weight of the body.

Index